DEMONS ARE REAL

Karee Gayle
Demons Are Real

Published by Spines
ISBN: 979-8-89383-518-2

DEMONS ARE REAL

NOT JUST CALLED, BUT CHOSEN

KAREE GAYLE

CHAPTER 1

BATTLING DEMONS

A JOURNEY OF FAITH AND SPIRITUAL WARFARE

I was born in a religious family and raised in the city of West Palm Beach, Florida. I am one of seven children and the middle child. As a child, I always saw demons in various forms: sometimes as women, men, insects, and animals. During my childhood, I was fearful at times when I saw spirits. During bedtime, I tucked my head under the covers to keep from seeing beyond the natural. The evil spirits always appeared in physical form and in my dreams, but there were times when I saw angels of God, which were of a different countenance. The angels of God were very bright, peaceful, and comforting in comparison to the demons.

Growing up was not easy but very miserable. There were times that I became suicidal and consumed an excessive amount of whatever pills were within my reach to numb my emotional pain. Once I made it to age eleven, I constantly prayed for God to take me to heaven. Not long after the age of twelve, I ran away from home, thinking that I might obtain the results that I thought would work. A lack of trusting others and experiencing low self-esteem was the norm due to my trauma. After I became an adult and left home, my life became fifty times worse. I began to experience indescribable continuous demonic encounters and attacks. I was often approached by demons who threatened me by telling me that they were going to kill me. Not only was I being approached but followed. There were moments when I wondered if other people could see the spirits as they followed me.

A few years ago, one of the evil spirits that kept following me told me that I was a threat to his kingdom and that I must not interfere with whatever they had going on. Anyway, I wasn't afraid because I was used to seeing them throughout my childhood. However, there were times I wondered why I had to deal with this situation. "Is it that God wanted me to learn or study demonology?" "Is my purpose to cast out demons out of others?" Or "Am I supposed to spiritually help others?" I didn't really understand the situation until now. I was so miserable, wanting to die all the time as a way out of these situations.

A few years after my first demonic attack, I ate a meal that was prepared by someone who I knew, or thought I knew, well. Months after having eaten the meal, I experienced unusual weight gain, and weight loss, and became extremely ill. Shortly afterward, I was in and out of the hospital for at least twelve years. Most of the time, the doctors weren't able to give me an accurate diagnosis. Thankfully, I was raised in Christianity.

There were deliverance services on Sundays and Monday evenings during that time. I went to a service on a Sunday and a Monday evening where the presence of God was richly detected. The services on those evenings were so powerful that I knew something was going to happen to me. As the services drew closer to the end, I felt a powerful anointing that I'd never experienced until then. I found myself at the altar, vomiting on towels that were placed. Whatever it was that came out of my stomach was not pleasant and indescribable. It was definitely abnormal and horrifying to watch. However, I felt better physically after those services, which I call my breakthrough.

Prior to my breakthrough, many times I've heard demons communicating from within my stomach, both male and female voices. I couldn't believe that I was existing through these horrible experiences. Several years after vomiting out demons, I took off to the state of Connecticut to work. It so happened that a warlock was working at the same place I left Florida to work. He befriended me but a few months later decided to do all manner of evil to me. This co-worker was sending demons in the form of animals to attack me to the point of waking up in severe pain. He performed many demonic sacrificial performances in order to decrease my success and my spiritual relationship with God. He tried to destroy my success, inflicted pain physically, tried to separate me from everyone that was of support, and tried to afflict and oppress me in every way that he could. This person is someone who I also assisted financially and emotionally during his experiences of illness and depression. Just before he became my enemy, he told me that he would always be a part of my life, but I didn't understand what he meant at the time when he told me those words.

This man shows up in my dreams while I'm awake. He has also performed demonic sacrifices that kept witches and other warlocks following me everywhere I would go. If I tried to accomplish anything that was of success, he always tried to hinder or block any progress from manifesting. I wasn't able to keep a phone without him being able to hack, listen, and monitor all of my activities, and he made sure I knew he was on to me in every way. It wasn't just this warlock, but there were others who he recruited to try to destroy my life. No matter how many phones I purchased with new numbers and emails, it didn't stop these witches or warlocks from fighting against me. They would even end up with my client's phone numbers and Wi-Fi information. They would call my client's phones to release their demonic blows, attacks, and assignments that would dismiss my contracts and relationships with my clients.

The main motive of my enemies is to destroy the functionality of my mind. Each time that I used my phone or phones, I realized that I became very forgetful and was unable to think logically or comprehend. As I used my phones, their powers penetrated to the point of instant dizziness, which caused me to become forgetful, light-headed, and lacking in the ability to concentrate or comprehend. There is so much more to share. I wish these experiences were a dream but they are as real as life. I overcame these evils because of my faith in God. There were times that I wanted to just die; I've cried many days and nights.

I was extremely upset with God for having allowed me to experience this intense trauma. I kept praying, fasted, and encouraged others because I felt better when I did. I read the Bible, but another important thing that I found myself doing during those times was speaking to those situations by telling them that they don't exist! Every time I felt the intensity of the pain from these demonic attacks, I spoke with power and authority, rebuking and letting the demons, witches, and warlocks know that they don't, nor will they ever, obtain power or authority over my life or anything that concerns my life. I didn't used to understand that the mind is a powerful thing, but now I do! I now also understand how important it is for us as human beings to obtain and maintain a relationship with the man upstairs! Witches and warlocks are everywhere today. They look like normal people, so we can't tell from the natural eye who is who. Due to my past experiences, I implore everyone to be vigilant and careful of the people we invite into our lives and into our personal space. Today, I understand my purpose and reason for having endured such horrifying and traumatic experiences. The bigger one's purpose is, the bigger the warfare!

CHAPTER 2

TRACKED BY DARKNESS

ENDURING SPIRITUAL WARFARE AND FINDING PURPOSE

The warlock that lives in the state of Connecticut had a spiritual tracking device implanted in my left shoulder as a way of keeping track of wherever I went. Many times I felt a tingling in my left shoulder, which alerted me that I was being tracked. He did this to be able to send evil spirits and demonic blows wherever I would be. This warlock constantly sent attacks in the form of pain and disruption, affecting those around me. Sometimes other people who were within my environment felt the effects of the powers of evil but were not able to understand or explain what they were experiencing, which caused them to become frustrated! Due to the tracking device that was implanted in my left shoulder, the witches would call the phones of any public businesses where I went, such as restaurants, nail salons, department stores, etc. When their phone calls were answered, I knew because I immediately felt the effects of the forces of evil attacking my head. During those moments, I left in haste to prevent the forces from strengthening against my head. Another level of evil that I have experienced is not being able to sit on any cushion, nor was I able to sleep on a bed without experiencing the intensity of a continuous vibration. The vibrational effect was supposed to make me very uncomfortable and cause mental issues. After getting out of bed, most of the time I felt extremely light-headed and forgetful. The effect was almost as if I had a hangover. As soon as I had the chance, I read a few chapters in the Bible, the Book of Psalms. I read until the feeling that I was experiencing disappeared. In order for me to sleep while dealing with this situation, I had to use a Bible as a pillow to prevent waking up with such horrible feelings. This specific demon also tried to have sex with me at times. Prior to this situation, I had a vision in which I saw the witches and warlocks performing sacrificial rituals by killing animals for this specific evil spirit to continuously follow and attack me. Most of these demonic encounters and attacks were through blood-sacrificial performances! It didn't matter where I went; the same situations occurred. They went wherever I went. This season of affliction and oppression lasted for five years. During these years, other people approached me, seeking encouragement because of their struggles and hardships. While strengthening people who came, I also gained strength, but they had no idea of the circumstances that I was enduring. Fortunately, I laid my burdens aside with God-given strength in order to help those who were facing various struggles! When a one-on-

one session was completed, the tears from my eyes flowed like a water faucet. The angels of the Lord showed me many visions of my earthly purpose. A few years ago, there was a man with a bright countenance who appeared in front of me in a vision and held a conversation with me about my future. He then asked me, "Who will go?" I responded by telling him that I would go. After waking from such a powerful vision, I knew that I was about to enter a world of hell, and I did! As the warfare in my life became intense, an angel of God appeared again and asked me, "How can you help others if you've never experienced what they have been through, or similar circumstances?" When this angel asked me this question, I was becoming faithless, angry, disappointed, and wanted to give up! However, every time I felt like throwing in the towel, my conscience got the best of me, especially when I thought about those who were in need of spiritual assistance. I don't want to be one of those who were placed here on earth with a great purpose but refuse to accomplish what God has placed me here to do. I just don't want to live selfishly!

CHAPTER 3
NAVIGATING SPIRITUAL MINEFIELDS
TRIALS AND TRIUMPHS ON THE PATH TO LIBERATION

I was in search of help to overcome this situation during these trying times. I decided to attend a service outside of the United States at a particular time. On the third day of my visit, I realized that I made a mistake in attending the service. Most of the people who served ministry as ministers were involved in witchcraft! One of the witches who worked within the ministry sent an attack against my feet, causing my feet to swell to the point where I couldn't wear my shoes. Upon my departure, I was forced to purchase a pair of beach slippers that were much bigger and longer than my feet in order to travel back home. I was in awe that this happened to me. Also, I discovered that there was a curse placed upon my life to become a target, being approached and attacked by evil. Anywhere I went, it followed me. I have traveled to a few states to work, and everywhere I went there was always at least one person who came after me to harm me. At one point, I worked at an autism/disability camp as a co-supervisor. I was contracted to one year of work. At the beginning of my employment, the director became fond of me until the seventh month.

He became my enemy by turning everything that I did into a problem and more! Even if the tasks were correctly done, he made everything an issue. He began to watch me more than the norm, yelled at me unnecessarily, and communicated with an attitude. However, not long after the change in our relationship began, I saw him in my dreams doing some of the same things that other warlocks had done to me. I was on my way out the door one morning to begin work. I happened to look down at my doorstep and saw an unusual object lying there. The second I saw it, I knew that it was an evil assignment. I didn't use my bare hands to touch it. I picked up a shovel, but I prayed prior to removing it.

A few days later, I noticed that the sidewalk where I normally walked outside of the building appeared extremely bright, with x's all over, only once the sun was shining. I thought, how strange! There wasn't any object with the form or shape of an X, so I was a bit puzzled by what I saw for weeks. I was the only person who saw them. From then, I knew that I was in for another warfare. I went to the pool on-site one day, but something was strange about the water. Anyway, I went in the water, and the minute I made it in, my feet immediately became extremely weak and my whole body was jittery. On the opposite end of the pool, I saw spirits rising up within the water. They had disfigured and angry faces. Seconds later, I began to make my way out of the water. On my way out of the pool, I stepped on tiny sharp objects that felt almost like needles. Unfortunately, one of the needle-like objects got into my right foot and remained there for a while. There were times that I tried to use a safety pin to uproot whatever it was, but I had no luck trying that method. The more I dug, the more pain and burn I felt. While the object remained in my foot, I wasn't able to walk normally because my foot felt like it was on fire at times. I was in this situation for a year and seven months. One day, I woke up and realized that the discomfort and burning had stopped. It just mysteriously disappeared!

Once I became completely knowledgeable of the circumstances that I was faced with, I decided to bring my DVD player to my workstation and listen to numerous prayers and the reading of the Bible each day. Both the director and his assistant were very uncomfortable and became extremely miserable when they heard the prayers. They couldn't stand to hear it play, so the situation grew worse. But I continued to listen to the prayers and the reading of the Bible, which definitely helped! If the prayers and Bible weren't being played, I had massive headaches, unusual pain, panic attacks, dizziness, and more. A few months later, I quit because the battles were increasing by the day. Also, if I had given notice of my resignation, I knew that leaving would have been more of a struggle. The director tried many times to coax me to remain by renewing my contract in spite of the negativities he and his assistant were doing to me.

CHAPTER 4
EMBRACING PURPOSE
A JOURNEY THROUGH SPIRITUAL WARFARE AND HEALING

If I was not located by the witches and warlocks, within 20 minutes of being out of their presence, my feet burned as if they were on fire. They needed to know my exact location 24 hours a day, 7 days a week. Then, once they located me, the witches poked me sometimes on my back, arms, neck, and legs. At times, the effects of the pokes were more painful than at other times. The spirits would also groan if they weren't happy with whatever decisions I made that they found to be displeasing, such as when I prayed, worshipped, read the Bible out loud, encouraged others, called the name of Jesus, or mentioned the blood of Jesus. Also, when I went to church where the presence of God was felt or invoked! When I laughed loudly, it made them really upset. I didn't care; I did what I felt the need to do, whether the demons liked it or not. Because the evil spirits had so much control over my phones, I was not able to listen to or watch any media on my phone because of the effects on my head that caused dizziness or lightheadedness. I purchased a DVD player in order to listen to music, prayers, and the reading of the King James Bible. The demons tried to infuse my DVD player with the same level of evil effects that were experienced by my phones. Ever so often, I applied a bit of holy or anointing oil on my DVD player while it was in use. Had I not done so, I felt the same effects against my head from my other devices while in use. There was another warlock that was assigned to follow me everywhere I went. The smell of that spirit was not a pleasant one. His scent was like a mixture of cigarettes and marijuana, so I smelt him a mile away, which was very annoying and embarrassing because other people were able to smell him as well and probably thought that I was smoking either of the two.

I have lived most of my life in regret of being born. I remember praying at the age of 10 and 11, asking God to not allow me to wake up to see the next day. There were times that I was on the school bus during my elementary school years praying for the bus to crash so that I might die. I despised my life. I had a hard time learning effectively in school because all I could think about was the trauma that I dealt with on a daily basis. At times, I noticed other children, even my family members, and wished that I were able to trade places with them. I didn't think that I would have made it to my adult life. Sometimes I wonder how in the world I made it to see today.

Life is never easy for anyone who is truly chosen by Almighty God! To be called is one thing, but to be chosen is another. I remember being tempted during these trials to see witch doctors or voodoo priests to help me be healed or delivered from these severe demonic circumstances. There were times that I was out running errands and ran into psychics who stopped me to tell me what they saw happening in my life and gave me various advice concerning my issues. However, though I pondered the advice that was given, I knew that wasn't the way that the Lord wanted me to go. God's word tells us that He is a jealous God and that He doesn't want us to yield to serving other gods besides Him. If you read about many of the Bible characters who were chosen by God, you'll discover that they didn't have an easy way of life. They met many challenges that could have cost them their lives. I pray that my experiences will help other people to be delivered and overcome their hardships. What also helped me to overcome this is using the word of God to destroy the works of the enemy. Each time I felt an attack, I spoke these words: "YOUR POWERS WERE DESTROYED OVER TWO THOUSAND YEARS AGO THROUGH THE POWER OF THE BLOOD OF JESUS!" Though at times I had become tired of repeating myself, it was effective. The devil cannot stand to hear such words, not sentences! Words are indeed powerful! I began to put these words into the atmosphere after seeing a dream of an angel who appeared in front of me and spoke these words. I also remembered that my family members who are ministers taught the church to speak these powerful words and sentences as a way to hinder the attacks of Satan from manifesting.

Our purpose is sometimes delayed in order to protect us. I struggled with accepting this fact for a while. God sees and knows everything about our future. Satan also knows enough to try to throw stumbling blocks in our way to stop or block us from fulfilling our purpose, especially if our purpose is to help guide others. The enemy, which is Satan, will also try to kill us once he sees and understands how effective our destiny is or can be. So I have learned and have accepted the fact that purpose delays aren't always negative but sometimes turn out to be a positive thing! God's ways are totally different from our ways; likewise, his timing is definitely not always our timing. For these reasons, it is very imperative to develop a relationship with God. Seek His face by reading his words, praying constantly asking for his guidance, understanding, and wisdom. Ask God to reveal your purpose if you're not sure why you are here. It definitely helps to know or understand what our earthly purpose is! I have also learned that if we are living without fulfilling our true purpose, our lives will be cut shorter. Think about this, why am I here or what kind of effectiveness am I distributing while living? Honestly, it doesn't make sense to be here if we're not manifesting what God has placed us here for. Also, if we have met the level of perfection, there's no need for our lives to be prolonged! Let's take these thoughts into consideration and, most importantly, ask our heavenly father for guidance to fulfill our God-given purpose effectively and in a positive manner!

As far as my past relationships, most of the men I've dated were also in spiritual bondage but not as severely as I was. I worked as a caregiver for a few years which also helped with my healing process. During my time as a Patient Care Assistant, I had many opportunities to encourage and received words of encouragement and wisdom from the elderly. God allowed me to see visions of the end of life of some of those I cared for which he led me to pray with prior to their death. Even though life wasn't easy, there were amazing journeys of events that God himself brought me through which were mind-blowing and helpful in my healing process. I've also had the opportunity to facilitate group meetings in a few drug and alcohol rehab centers. With the help of the Lord, I was able to create a positive impact on the lives of most of the clients. A few, I lost to drug overdose during this journey which also taught me that we as humans cannot save others. We can only try; it takes the power of God to truly save us! This position gave me a chance to share my life experiences with the clients which they found to be extremely interesting. I was often asked, "How did you manage to miss being in rehab after all that you had been through?" My response to them was that it was only through the grace of God that I missed being in rehab, a mental hospital, and my grave! As I administered therapy, I was also being healed which amazed me during each session. During this period, I also discovered that our experiences and testimonies are not only for the strengthening of our faith but also to help others who may have dealt with the same or similar circumstances. In such a case, I am happy that I've been through such powerful experiences to share and to strengthen others but I definitely would not want to relive my past!

I recall praying one day in my living room until a tall angel appeared with a cane or what looked like a cane with a very bright countenance! That was another moment of indescribable peace that I didn't want to leave me. I prayed at that moment until I found myself crying hysterically and begging that angel not to leave after being with me for a while. I had never thought that I could experience such visitations from the angels of God! I asked myself many times, what is it about me that I could have the presence of angels approach or appear within my environment or come near me for that matter? I have questioned myself asking who am I, I'm only human, I'm far from being perfect but that's an answer that could only come from Almighty God himself I thought! I don't always have an answer nor am I able to explain 'a lot of things. However, I do know that God, his angels, and demons are very real! I also know that God is to be acknowledged, honored, and served wholeheartedly. I am only human who is far from being perfect but I have made up my mind to at least try to please the Lord by doing his will. I want to be sure that I am fulfilling my godly purpose effectively and positively! Hence, I encourage you to try to do the same so that all will go well with you. Christianity on a whole is not always easy nor is it a walk in the park but maintaining a relationship with the man upstairs is what strengthens us and helps us to endure this journey! We are also here to be of assistance to each other by keeping one another encouraged and strengthened. When our lives have come to an end, we want to hear, "Well done thou good and faithful Servant." Not "depart from me, I know you not!" I hope someone becomes elated, strengthened, and educated by my testimony. I thought long and hard about writing my story because I thought maybe they wouldn't even believe that any could have gone through such intense and severe situations. I never thought that anyone could possibly endure such issues! If I were told as a child or a teenager that I was going to face these circumstances I wouldn't have believed it. I didn't even think that there was an existing God. I guess it took dealing with these horrifying experiences for me to understand that there is a God and that there is a spiritual world that does exist and always has!

CHAPTER 5

INHERITING THE MANTLE

CONTINUING THE LEGACY OF SPIRITUAL WARFARE

My grandfather was a mighty warrior in ministerial warfare. He too experienced many demonic battles during his lifetime especially while raising his children. Many people received their deliverance through the anointing and power of God that was upon his life! My grandfather was feared by many who knew him demons also feared him. He was so powerful that wherever his presence was evil spirits literally ran, vanished, and fled. There are so many who are able to share testimonials of their demonic breakthrough and deliverance through the ministry of my grandfather! After the passing of my grandfather, I stood at his burial crying. As I was crying, I heard a voice saying don't cry. Your grandfather wouldn't want you to cry but to carry on with what he didn't finish. I didn't quite understand exactly what that meant because I was a bit younger and immature spiritually. Prior to his passing, I called him to pretty much say goodbye because I knew that he was about to die. As our conversation was about to end, these were his final words: "MAY THE GOD OF HEAVEN KEEP YOU PROTECTED FROM ALL EVIL AND BLESSED AS YOU CARRY ON"! Immediately I began to weep uncontrollably. I didn't even understand why I wept as much as I did but apparently, he knew why. I now understand what I didn't uncontrollably then. A few years later, I went to visit a ministry in another state. During the midst of the service, a prophet called me out of the crowd and prophesied to me by telling me that when my grandfather passed away, he dropped the mantle on me that he was carried throughout his life as Elijah the prophet dropped his mantle on Elisha as he was ascending into the heavens in a chariot. Which is why I was dealing with so many demonic battles. Once again I wept because I knew that prophecy was true. Certainly, I was going through a rough time spiritually. As far as being called out by prophets, it happened almost at every ministry I visited where the prophetic anointing was. No matter how I tried to hide in the crowd of a prophetic ministry, I was always spotted, called out, and prophesied with the same prophetic words! There were times that I wish I were able to communicate with my grandfather to share with him how difficult of a time I was experiencing and that I wish I had the power to pass the mantle to someone else. Many days I asked why and just cried hysterically. However, I have now gotten over the hurdles and am now stronger, wiser, and more knowledgeable of the calling that is upon my life. I'm also now willing to allow God to use me for his purpose and glory!